# Transformational
# Mothering
## A Prayerful Companion for New Mothers

*Amy Robbins-Wilson*

ISBN: 978-0-578-00948-3
Library of Congress Control Number: 2009922829

Angelsong Creations, LLC
www.angelsongcreations.com

This book is given to:

With love from:

Transformational Mothering—A Prayerful

Companion for New Mothers

by Amy Robbins-Wilson

*Passages marked with a 🎼 indicate that they can also be sung. Visit www.transformationalmothering.com to receive a free download of the music.*

*The first time I ever idolized my mother,*
*she was peeling an egg.*

*She crushed and rolled it against the countertop,*
*carefully picked at one corner,*
*and it opened, revealing its perfect white center.*
*It was as if an angel had hatched in her hands.*

*I thought, "This is what it means to be a good mother."*
*You open things,*
 *reveal them,*
  *without breaking anything.*
*I thought,*
 *"Someday,*
  *when I can do that…*

*I will be a good mother, too."*

**I lovingly dedicate this book to my mother, Louine.**

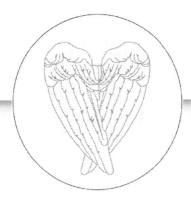

When we approach motherhood as a "job," we put ourselves at the service of our children.

If approached as a spiritual practice, we see it as a journey of mutual benefit. It becomes an adventure to be embarked upon with great anticipation and expectation, a pilgrimage of the soul.

We do not embark on great journeys expecting all to go smoothly. Schedules will not always be kept, not all roads will be easily traveled, but there will be learning in every step and joy in unexpected places.

We emerge transformed.

This is (wholly) holy sacred practice.

An Introduction

Motherhood was the first thing I knew I could not do without God. I first understood the meaning of unceasing prayer as I was rushed to the hospital and into an emergency cesarean birth due to a placental abruption. I knew the deep peace of the presence of God on that emergency room table, and I knew the presence of angels as my newborn son, Clayton, recovered in the neonatal intensive care unit (NICU). When we returned home, it was prayer that kept my anxiety from overwhelming me and my fears at bay. It was the presence of God that helped me up every two hours to nurse and later through another hospital emergency. Now it is prayer that sustains me.

Motherhood is my spiritual practice. That first year with my baby transformed me in ways I could not have previously imagined. In that year I celebrated my new baby, I mourned my previous life, I was tried and I was tested. I was the happiest I had ever been and the most lost.

As a new mother I was often encouraged to look at mothering as my new "job." I frequently heard: "Motherhood is the hardest job you will ever love," and, "Motherhood is the hardest, best job in the world."

I read about mothers who called themselves the CEO of the home, and my first Mother's Day, mothers were all abuzz because salary.com had suggested a salary of between $165,000 and $185,000 a year for the job of "mother." Salaries varied based on the amount of cleaning, laundry, cooking, and caretaking done. There was even a check that could be printed out and given to mothers that read, "Mom, if I could, I would pay you…"

Though all well intentioned, giving mothers a fake check seemed to me to be a misunderstanding of the service of motherhood. We don't mother for the money. Our children are not a product of our job— they are our teachers, and they are sacred vessels of knowledge.

This book was born from my desire to see mothering as something other than work, a job, or a sacrifice. When in those other modes, I felt alternately like a fool working too hard for no pay and no benefits, a beast of burden, or a martyr. I struggled with my new identity until I realized that was exactly what I was supposed to be doing. I asked myself, "Is this postpartum depression?" But I was not depressed; I was transforming. As a wise friend pointed out, "Amy, you have gone from being an independent, energetic, adventurous, and self-sufficient person to being at home with your baby. You are not depressed; you are leaving your old life behind. You are on a new path now."

Becoming a mother is a rite of passage.

I share these prayers and this perspective on motherhood not because it is the only or the best way to mother, for it is neither of those things. I offer this book to women who wish to find a deeper sense of themselves and a deeper connection to God through their mothering. This practice will not guarantee that your children will behave better than others or be any smarter or even that they will sleep through the night. What I pray that this practice will do is reassure you that you are not alone and that there is always someone to turn to in prayer.

I consider my first year of mothering my initiation period. It was a time of transformation between what I once was and what I was becoming. Small rituals and prayers began to transform the trying times of motherhood into times of worship. The gift of a night-light with Mother Mary holding her son on it was a call to transformation. Nursing by this small light made a dramatic difference in how I saw our time together. My baby's cry became my call to worship. These times were our "night-light services."

Our daily services slowly settled down into a peaceful and predictable rhythm as I observed the divine hours of motherhood. Each evening this small night-light and lullabies marked our Vespers service as I called the angels down to watch over my baby as he slept. Compline was spent with my husband talking about our day. Clayton's cry was my call to Vigils during the night and my call to Lauds in the morning, where I praised God for the beauty of my boy, for he is wondrously made. At Terce, Sext, and None, I worshiped by feeding, cleaning, tending, and laughing with my baby.

Even today my prayers are constant. *Dear God, please help me to be a good mother. Dear God, please give me patience. Dear God, in a world of high fructose corn syrup, di-this and monounsaturated-that, please help me to make healthy food choices for my family. Dear God, please open my heart to Your love that it may stream forth into my family and into the world.*

Many nights as I sang and rocked Clayton to sleep, I recalled similar services many years ago where in a pink bedroom illuminated by a light from under the door and a lullaby, I rocked safely in the arms of my mother. I could feel her touch as I reached out to caress my own son in his sleep, and I said a grateful prayer for my mother and for my son. For they have taught me that a paycheck can never be the measure of a mother's worth, that it can be a blessing to be caught up in the whirlwind, that every day is a sacred event, and that the depths of a mother's love are unfathomable.

Love and blessings on your journey,
Amy Robbins-Wilson

*Note: Whenever I write about mothering, I think of my son. I have chosen to use the pronoun "he" throughout this book as it is how I most naturally write and is easier to read than he/she or "child."*

Dear God,

I ask Your blessing upon this book and all who
    read it.

May it illuminate our hearts and minds and inspire
    us to turn toward prayer.

May it lessen our judgments and connect us
    to each other.

May we know deep in our hearts that there is no
    single way to raise our children.

May we know that we bless all children when we
    bless those who raise them.

May we be guided by You each and every moment
    in this transformational journey called
    motherhood.

This is too big for us without You, Lord.

Thank You for being here.

When we are fearful, send us Your angels of calm.

When we are uncertain, clear our minds.

When we are impatient, breathe into us the wonder
    of the moment.

Open our hearts, Lord, as we read and as we live.

Thank You.

Amen.

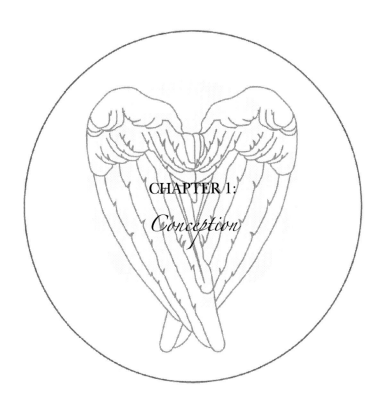

CHAPTER 1:

*Conception*

CONCEPTION:
(from www.thefreedictionary.com)

**a.** Formation of a viable zygote by the union of the male sperm and female ovum; fertilization.

**b.** Something conceived in the mind; a concept, plan, design, idea, or thought.

**c.** *Archaic* A beginning; a start.

In my twenties, I was sure that I would have children one day. In my early thirties, I was quite sure I would not. It was only when I saw my then-fiancé, Tim, tenderly caring for a crazed feral kitten that I felt my call to be a mother.

We conceive of our children in many different ways. Some we pray for; others surprise us. Some are brought to us through our own pregnancies and some by the pregnancies of others. Conceiving the idea of having children and physically conceiving may be closely linked in time or drawn out over heartbreaking months or years. Responses to pregnancy can range from all-consuming joy to overwhelming fear.

I remember the crisp, clear fall day when, after months of taking temperatures and keeping calendars, I hiked up the hill in the back of the apartment complex where we were living—to pray. The sun filtered down through the trees as I sat on a rock, closed my eyes, and asked God and the angels to surround me and help me to conceive. In my mind's eye, I glimpsed a little boy running around me, and when I opened my eyes, there were three deer standing only feet from where I sat.

I felt that my prayer had been answered and that we would soon be a family of three. A few days later, two pregnancy tests came back positive, and we were ecstatic. I looked in the mirror, hand on my belly, and said, "I am going to be your mom." What a miracle.

A Prayer for a Healthy Pregnancy and Baby

Dear God,
We believe that we are ready to share our love and
    our lives with a child.
Please bless us with a healthy pregnancy and the
    peaceful birth of the child You would have us raise.
We are so excited at the thought of being parents!
Please surround us with Your loving light and
    help us to conceive easily.
What a miracle that life might be created though us.
Prepare us for this incredible journey, Lord.
Hear our prayer.
Lead our lives.
Thank You.
Amen.

### A Prayer for When Pregnancy is a Surprise

Dear God,

I am in shock.

This is not what I had planned.

I feel uncertain, unsure, and overwhelmed.

Grant me Your wisdom and understanding, Lord.

Surround me with friends whom I can count on
during this time.

I give You my fears. I ask for Your peace.

I give You my uncertainty. I ask for Your grace.

Help me to choose this child.

Help me to plan my way forward with joy.

I cannot do this without You, Lord.

I am so grateful that I do not have to.

Thank You.

Amen.

A Prayer When Disappointed at Not Being Pregnant

Dear God,

I just found out that I am not pregnant.

I feel so deeply, incredibly disappointed and sad.

Help me to trust the process of my life.

Wrap Your love around me and grant me
     peace and patience.

I know that I will be a mother soon.

I see myself radiantly healthy and holding my
     beautiful baby.

Today, I embrace all that I have and renew my faith
     in what I am about to receive.

Be with me, Lord.

Thank You.

Amen.

## A Prayer for When Conceiving is Difficult

Dear God,

This path I am on feels life-consuming
and disappointing.

I want so much to be a mother.

It seems eons that I have been controlled by
calendars, temperatures, and tests.

Guide me, Lord.

Help me to know which paths to pursue in my quest
to be a mother.

I ask that You open my heart to inspired
conversations with those who can help me.

I ask that You open doors to the tests and
procedures that will serve our family best.

Speak to my heart, Lord.

If it is for the highest and greatest good that I
become a mother, I ask that You make my
way clear.

I am so grateful to know You are with me.

Thank You.

Amen.

A Prayer for Undergoing In Vitro Fertilization

Dear God,

I ask Your blessing on this process.

Please bless the doctors and nurses, the technicians,
and the labs that are helping us to make our
family possible.

Bless all those who have developed
these procedures.

Bless the medicines involved and those who
created them.

Watch over me, Lord, as I assimilate the medicines
necessary for this process.

Make me a vessel of Your light, Lord.

What a miracle that life might be formed and
shaped within me.

Be with me, Lord.

Be my guide.

Thank You.

Amen.

A Prayer for Dealing with Infertility

Dear God,

I have been told that I will not be able to
carry a child.

My heart is breaking, Lord.

I feel broken beyond repair.

I know that I am being called to be a mother.

Show me the path You would have me walk toward
the family I will one day have.

Hold me in your heart, Lord.

Speak to me.

Lead me on.

Thank You.

Amen.

## A Prayer When Considering Adoption

Dear God,

We have so much love to give.

We ask that You bless us with Your guidance.

We are considering adopting a child.

Please open our hearts to all possibilities.

Send us advisors and angels to point us
> in the right direction.

Still our fears and grant us patience.

We know that there will be a child in our life
> when the time is right.

We are so anxious to meet him.
> Please guide him to our side.

Make us a family.

Thank You, Lord.

Amen.

CHAPTER 2:

*Pregnancy*

The first time I felt Clayton move, it was nothing like the "butterflies" I'd read about. He felt like a ball rolling over in my belly. I was awestruck. Pregnancy took on a whole new dimension once I could feel our baby move.

I kept a journal during my pregnancy, and I love to read it now that Clayton is here. It is amazing to me how his behavior in utero foretold the little person I have come to know. Clayton was quite mellow, even in the womb. With the exception of some kicks to the chest, he was not overly active. He stayed high in the womb during most of my pregnancy and was to be born before he had time to "drop."

As with his birth, he seems to reach for milestones before I am prepared for him to be there; so far, we have made it through. His quiet strength and joy of life continue to surprise and enchant me. At two, he still likes to curl up high on my chest, and I love having him so close to my heart.

## A Prayer for Healthy Habits

Dear God,

I ask Your guidance in making healthy choices for
    my baby and me.

Help me to crave nutritious foods and inspire me to
    do what I need to do to prepare my body for birth.

Any unhealthy habits I have been holding onto,
    I release to You, Lord.

Take them and transform them.

As my body is being transformed,
    transform also my soul.

Make me a vessel for Your love, Lord.

Thank You.

Amen.

## A Prayer for When There Are Complications

Dear God,

Please still my fears.

There are complications with this pregnancy that
no one could have anticipated.

Be with me now.

Grant me wise counsel as I make decisions related
to this new situation.

Hold my baby in the golden light
of Your love.

Hold me in the palm of Your hand.

Thank You.

Amen

## A Prayer for Release from Worry

Dear God,

I know that worry will not add a minute to my life.

Yet my mind is full and spinning endlessly.

Please still my fears.

Send Your angels of peace to wrap their wings
around me and comfort me.

Bless my baby, Lord.

Bless me as I change and as I grow.

Thank You.

Amen.

A Prayer for Guidance

Dear God,

As I talk with people and read about this upcoming
    birth, I am overwhelmed by the choices placed
    before me.

Guide me, Lord.

Inspire my thoughts, my conversations,
    and my decisions.

Please, God, make my path clear so that this child
    may be welcomed to my side in the healthiest
    and most joyful way.

Thank You.

Amen.

## A Prayer of Gratitude

Dear God,

I feel so blessed and grateful to be having this child.

Thank You for this incredible gift.

I ask that You prepare me for all that lies ahead.

Keep us healthy and fill me with Your peace.

Be by my side as I embark upon this great journey.

Walk with me, Lord.

Make my way clear.

All things are possible with You by my side.

Thank You.

Amen.

## A Prayer When Expecting Twins

Dear God,

I know now that I am carrying twins.

I am so excited and so nervous!

Strengthen me, Lord.

Prepare me.

When I am feeling overwhelmed, bring Your light
and love around me.

When I am feeling joy, celebrate with me.

When I am struggling, bring me to rest
in Your arms.

Help me to raise these children to be the light-filled
beings You would have us all become.

Thank You very much.

Amen.

## A Prayer for Physical Wellness

Dear God,

When I feel tired, lift me up.

When I am feeling sick, Lord, fill me with the
light of love and healing.

Send Your sweetest angels to watch over me
and my baby.

Help me to sleep soundly and deeply,
cradled in Your arms.

Thank You.

Amen.

---

*Remember to breathe.*
*Your child learns how to breathe from you.*

---

A Prayer for Guidance through the Adoptive Process

Dear God,
What a miracle that our child has been born
    or will soon be born into this world!
Help us to find him, Lord.
When we have doubts, calm our minds.
When we have decisions to make, be our guide.
Lead us, Lord, through the labyrinth
    that will unite us with our child.
We ask Your blessing on all involved
    in the creation of our family.
Bless them.
Bless us.
May this process be led by the light of Your love.
Thank You.
Amen.

---

*All decisions can be divinely guided.*
*Ask, and doors will be opened.*

---

Adoption is a magical process. The stories of how children are united with their parents are amazing and attest to the astounding guidance God can provide when our hearts are open. Children conceived in this way are held in our hearts until they are held in our arms.

> *Blessed be the ties that bind.*
> *Blessed be the ties that bind our hearts.*
> *Blessed be the ties that bind our hearts*
> *in human love.*
> *Blessed be the ties that bind us.*
> *Lord, bind us,*
> *for we are bound in beauty.*

The adoptive process is a kind of pregnancy of paperwork—a true "labor of love." Organizing home visits, scheduling time with agencies, filling out paperwork—the decisions can be daunting. Will you take a special-needs child? Will you adopt a child of a different race? Will you adopt internationally? Will the birth mother have rights of contact? As with any pregnancy, it can be a roller coaster filled with joys and setbacks.

*I am divinely protected and supported in every moment.*

During the adoption process, prayer can serve as a way to focus your intentions and guide the way forward. Praying for a birth mother may entail praying for a woman who has already been identified, or it may include praying for her before she is known to you as a way of guiding her and your baby to you. Whether you know the birth mother of your child or not, prayer is a way to be connected to her and to your baby.

## A Prayer for a Birth Mother

Dear God,

Please bless the woman who is carrying our baby.

Inspire her to eat well and take good care of herself.

She is making our family possible,

   and I am so grateful.

Please Lord, send Your angels down around her.

Guide her day.

Bring her joy, peace, and great love.

Watch over all of us as we nurture each other and

   this new life.

We ask that You bless

   our child's birth mother, Lord.

Bless the life of this woman that she may

   move forward in grace and with

   Your guidance.

Bless us as we move toward being a family.

Thank You.

Amen.

CHAPTER 3:

*Becoming a Family*

We have no idea what we are capable of until we become mothers. Whether it is the pain of labor, the endless paperwork and bureaucratic frustrations of adoption, the scars of cesarean births, or the challenges of a sick child, we do what must be done.

"Are you feeling okay, Amy?" asked my birthing class instructor after explaining what happens in a cesarean birth. "You look a little green."

"I think I can endure just about any pain as long as I do not have to deal with those needles," I replied. I was thirty weeks pregnant, I had read shelves full of books, and my husband and I had taken HypnoBirthing® classes. We had a birth plan! We had a doula! We were prepared! When my doctor said, "Just remember that the only thing that really matters is a healthy baby and a healthy mother," I was not convinced. I wanted to have the "right" kind of birth. I still believed I was in control.

Four weeks later, in rural Maine, a different doctor said to me, "Amy, you have a decision to make. You can have a cesarean here or in Bangor. If you try to make it to Bangor, your baby probably will not survive. You have one minute to decide." Seconds later, I was being wheeled into the operating room to deliver my baby boy five and a half weeks early. The only thing that mattered to me then was that he and I lived. It was the perfect birth to teach me the power of surrender. All I could do was breathe deeply and pray.

Until I was a mother, I did not truly understand what it meant to live a life of service, and I did not understand the difference between service and sacrifice.

Looking in from the outside, much of what others considered sacrifice I learned to consider service. For example, nursing my son every two hours served us both. When I was tired, however, giving up time to sit and read by myself often felt like a sacrifice. I learned to see this feeling of sacrifice as a signal that I needed a break to recharge.

Gifts given with great love and without expectation are channels for the Divine. In serving my child, I know that I am not doing this alone; I am a vessel for grace. It is not about how people see me as a mother; it is about how I am able to open myself and my family, revealing them without breaking anything.

We soak in the blessings, we witness the mystery and the miracles, we rise to the challenges, and we pray.

*Dear God, I am a mother now. Please, hear my prayer.*

## A Prayer for Birth

Dear God,

Be with us now.

Send Your great and glorious angels down around
us and bathe us in Your light.

The time has come to welcome this new child into
our arms and into our lives.

Please bless the hands of these doctors and nurses.

Please bless us all with Your peace
and clear thinking.

Bless this body that housed this new being,
this old soul.

We feel the presence of Your love and the
joyful excitement of this little one.

Please help guide and prepare our son
as he transforms from pure spirit
to embodied light.

These moments—all moments—are sacred, Lord.

Wrap us in Your love.

Open our hearts that we might illuminate the world
through Your example.

We are blessed.

We are grateful.

Each breath we take reminds us how deeply we are
loved and how profoundly we are connected.

At this birth, may we all be reborn.

Thank You.

Amen.

Being a first-time mother is a leap into the unknown. Some mothers choose not to read anything, some mothers read everything they can get their hands on, some mothers welcome advice, and others actively avoid discussions on the topics of birth and motherhood. We all cope with our uncertainty in our own way.

I read voraciously, but ultimately, it was my angels and my intuition that prepared me and eventually saved my son and me. I was five months pregnant when the thought came to me, *If you ever see blood, you must rush yourself to the hospital.* It was as if it had been whispered in my ear. I quickly blocked the thought from my mind and convinced myself that this would never happen.

Later, in my birthing class, we were asked to draw a picture of what would get us through our labor. I drew my husband's eyes and then surrounded them with green for health and pink for love. I added a spiral on his forehead to connect him with God. When I stepped back, I was shocked to see that I had drawn the face of a doctor with a green surgical mask and a spiral where a headlamp would be. While my conscious self was preparing for a natural birth, I believe I was unconsciously being prepared for the reality of what was to come.

We were living in New Hampshire during our pregnancy. However, when the day came that I was having pain and feeling sick, I was visiting my family in Maine. I sat down and said, "Angels, I need a sign. If I need to go to the hospital, let me know." Seconds later I was bleeding, and I knew.

Looking back, I should never have hesitated to go in the first place. I was worried about co-pays and insurance, and I had never known anyone who had given birth so early. I didn't want to be seen as a spleeny pregnant woman, and it was not really a part of my consciousness that things could go any other way than what I had planned.

My birthing books told me that birth is to women what war is to men. They stressed that the birth experience was about me. They insinuated that it was about proving my competence to the world.

I have come to believe that birth is about surrender. Whether it is surrendering to the pain of labor, the necessity of paperwork, or the need for a cesarean, each birth offers us a chance to be reborn as mothers. My son has been my greatest teacher.

*I accept and respect the choices of others knowing that we are united in our struggles over the decisions of motherhood.*

*I respect that other mothers can make wise choices that are different from the choices I have made for my baby and me.*

A Prayer for Labor

*I am in the hands of God.*

Dear God,

You have given me this body as a perfect example
of Your grace.

Help me to trust it.

Take my fear and fill me with confidence.

May every discomfort open me more to this
blessing and to Your love.

I am Your vessel, Lord. Use me.

Bless the hands of all those who will be at this birth.

Bless us all with quick thinking and wisdom in the
face of any difficulty.

Surround us with Your light and Your love.

May this birth bless us all.

May it bless the world.

Thank You.

Amen.

## A Prayer for Meeting Your Child for the First Time (Adoption)

> *All things are in perfect process.*

Dear God,

I have waited so long for this day to come.

What a miracle that I am to be blessed with this
child to raise.

Please be with us all at this meeting.

Wrap us in the light of Your love
and understanding.

I am so full of emotion, Lord.

I am so blessed.

I ask Your guidance as we become a family.

Walk with us on this journey, Lord.

Make our paths clear.

Thank You.

Amen.

A friend, who adopted an older child internationally,
expressed to me how daunting it was to be the
instant mother of an eighteen-month-old. It
takes time to find a rhythm, and it is a challenge to
bond with your child while holding the boundaries

needed at that age. Getting home through airports, security, planes, trains and automobiles was a test, and people who did not understand the situation were not at all supportive.

## A Prayer for Adopting an Older Child

Dear God,

I feel so blessed to have finally found my child.

Thank You for the gift of my new family.

Please be with me now as I become a mother.

Lord, I have never done this before.

Please be with me on this journey.

My son and I have just met, yet the world expects
   us to be in a rhythm we have not yet
      had time to establish.

Be with us as we build a history together.

Help me to be accepting of my child and of myself
   as we grow together in Your love and
      understanding.

Send Your angels down around us.

Guide our day.

Guide our family.

Guide our life.

Thank You.

Amen.

## A Prayer of Thanks

Dear God,
My son is truly wondrously made.
I have never been as happy as I am
    in this moment, Lord.
Thank You for all of the joy being a mother
    brings to my life.
My heart has never felt such love.
I have never felt so blessed.
Thank You.
Amen.

While we all hope for an easy and direct route to motherhood, the truth is that the path is often winding and unpredictable with bends in the wood leading alternately to joy and to sorrow. When a child is lost either through miscarriage, a birth mother's change of heart, or stillbirth, there are no words. There is only prayer.

## A Prayer after a Loss

Dear God,

Our hearts are breaking.

We know now that the child we have held in our
hearts will not be ours to raise.

There are no words for this pain, Lord.

Be with us.

Guide and comfort us.

We ask Your special blessing upon the baby
we have lost.

Please welcome this small soul into Your
loving care.

Restore us, Lord.

Bless us and show us the way forward.

Thank You.

Amen

CHAPTER 4:

*Becoming a Mother*

Becoming a mother is not something for which we can prepare. It is the unknowable known, the mystery that must be circled rather than approached directly. When we embrace the profound transformation of motherhood, we see that we are not only in the service of our children, but of ourselves.

Our children are the teachers who open our hearts, who challenge our souls to grow, who transform us into who we are to become. This way of thinking shifts us from a place of resentment to a place of grace, and that grace is what blesses our homes, our families, and our lives.

A few months into motherhood, I tuned in to a television show featuring a mother of two young boys. The hosts, who are not parents themselves, were trying to assist this mother through a hard time by talking about how we as women should constantly seek to be in contact with our joy, our bliss, and our "natural vitality."

I know that my mental state at that time colored the way that I viewed the show. That said, I didn't know whether to laugh or cry or be furious that these childless co-hosts were preaching to this mother—and seemingly to me—about finding our bliss.

I was quite sure that the first year of motherhood was not about feeling vital. For me, still seriously sleep deprived, it was more about endurance. There were blissful moments, to be sure, and even days of sheer joy, but I was far from my best. Were other mothers actually able to be constantly joyful?

I felt like such a failure.

The mother in the program was obviously in need of more time to herself. She needed a larger support network and some time to regroup from all that she was giving. While the show's hosts supported her in moving forward in those goals, one vital piece seemed to be missing in their guidance. This mother needed to be honored. When talking to mothers about our lives, we must find a balance between discouraging martyrdom and honoring the service of motherhood.

When we as a society lose our sense of responsibility and the value of service to each other, motherhood is denigrated. In a world where you are supposed to do only what makes you feel comfortable or continuously "good," "happy," or "vital," the service of motherhood makes no sense.

It is only when I look at my life as a continuum, as a journey of growth and transformation, that I can understand motherhood, service, and joy. I trade the perpetual search for "happiness" for joy, "feeling good" for peace, and the endless search for "vitality" for profound connection and transcendence. From this new space of transformation and gratitude, I can see my mothering as a valuable and vital part of my life, of my community, and of my world.

## A Prayer for the Community of Mothers

Dear God,

I know that right now there are millions of women
     mothering their children.

Help me to feel connected to this network of miracles.

I am rooted in a line of mothers reaching back to the
     beginning of time and forward into eternity.

Lord, help me to feel this eternal thread.

Use it to bind me in love to all other mothers.

Though we may not agree on techniques, we share
     a common bond of love for our children.

May this love move through all of us and
     into the world.

May our love shine so brightly that our own hearts
     are filled and our children illuminated.

May our community of mothers bless the world.

Thank You.

Amen.

## A Prayer for Mothers Everywhere

Dear God,
I pray today for all mothers everywhere—
    for mothers who are struggling,
    for mothers who are overtired,
    for mothers who each and every moment
    reach deep inside themselves to draw upon endless
    wells of patience and caring
    despite all odds.
Wrap Your arms around us, Lord.
Send Your mightiest and gentlest angels
    to be our guides.
Open our hearts to Your infinite love that it might
    shine through us and light the world.
Thank You.
Amen.

Many mothers are single mothers raising their children. Whether this is by choice or the consequence of a divorce or death of a spouse, the following prayers are for you.

## A Prayer for the Mother Who Chooses
## Single Motherhood

Dear God,

I feel so blessed to have this child.

Help me to manage all that rides on my shoulders.

Help me to find a balance between

    work and mothering and guide me

    to those who would assist me.

I cannot do this alone, Lord.

Walk beside me.

Help me to find a loving and caring community.

Guide my hand.

Guide my life.

Thank You.

Amen.

## A Prayer for the Unmarried
## Single Mother

Dear God,

I cannot imagine sharing my baby.

My heart is so torn.

Help me to see my baby's life with his father as a
blessing rather than a burden.

I ask Your blessing on all those who are involved in
my baby's life.

May we work together easily to raise this child.

May our choices be guided by the love that we all
have for this little miracle.

May our past hurts be forgiven as we move forward
with You by our side.

Thank You, Lord.

Amen.

## A Prayer for the Mother Whose Husband Has Died

Dear God,

Holding together the love that I have for my child
    and the loss that I bear in my husband's death
    is almost too much for my body and soul
    to handle.

This is not what I had planned, Lord.

This is not what I would have chosen.

Be with me in every hour of this day.

Help me to find a community that loves and
    supports my baby and me.

Before me, Lord, I can see only
    the mountains I must climb.

Make my footsteps sure and strong;
    make my path clear.

I walk in beauty, Lord, when I walk in Your light.

I give my burdens to You.

I give You my grief and my mourning.

Grant me Your peace, Lord.

Where I am empty, fill me with Your love.

When I am lonely, hold me in Your arms.

There is no way but forward, Lord.

Please guide me.

Thank You.

Amen

CHAPTER 5:

*Feeding and the Body*

Breastfeeding may be natural, but it is not easy.
Pumping is no picnic, and formula can be an absolute
blessing. I pumped every three hours around the clock
during our time in the neonatal intensive care unit
(NICU). Any milk I was able to produce, my husband
would take to the nursery to be combined with
formula and coaxed into my son.

I know (and am related to) women who are blessed
with milk that flows freely and easily at the sound of
their baby's cry. Bless them and their breasts. It was
not so for me. I never had to worry about breast pads.
I never leaked. I drank my water and prayed that I
was producing enough milk to keep my baby healthy.
We supplemented with formula for months and I
took medication to get my milk supply up. Blissful
breastfeeding did not happen for us until Clayton
was at least four months old. It seemed that once
we got it all together, it was time to supplement
with cereal.

Mixing anything seemed dangerous. I had used ready-
made formula instead of powdered the entire time
we supplemented because I thought I might mix it
incorrectly; now I had to mix cereal? I kept putting
it off, but it was obvious when he was six months old

that he needed more than I could give him. I was absolutely, irrationally afraid of giving him solid food. Would it be the right cereal? Was it organic? Would I mix it right? Where would I feed him? Can a baby choke on pureed peas? Will he be allergic? If he was allergic, how would I tell? Peanut allergies seemed particularly scary. I made sure that the first time I gave my son peanut butter we were in a hospital parking lot. (He was almost two.)

Looking back, I was crazy to have worried so much, but being overtired and overwhelmed distorts all proportions. And who knows? Maybe it wasn't so crazy. As of this moment, my son is healthy and a good eater whose biggest food challenge is that he fills his mouth too full. I am not advocating worrying; as my husband constantly reminds me, "It will not add a single day to your life" (and it may just shorten his). However, balancing productive worry, which realistically keeps your child safe, with destructive worry, which repetitively mulls over scenarios that will never happen, is a continuous challenge in a new mother's life.

If cereal was enough to put me into a panic, you can only imagine the churnings that went on about

how and when to vaccinate. Suffice it to say that
my husband is a very patient man with amazing
research skills.

There is also the other body to think about—your
own. Though many women seem to bounce right back
into shape after birth, I was not one of those women.
I nursed until Clayton was eighteen months old.
Though nursing is often linked to weight loss, it was
not true for me. It took me eighteen months to lose
the baby weight and my breasts seem to have forgotten
that they were once a "C" and remain a "DD."

I wish I could tell you that I wouldn't trade my old
body for this one, that I see my stretch marks and
other scars as relics of my initiation. I am not there yet.
It has been said, "You teach what you need to learn."
I write what I need to pray. I am still learning and
growing. I am transforming. I am still building
my temple.

## A Prayer for Breastfeeding

Dear God,
Thank You for the miracle of breastfeeding.
Thank You for helping me to produce
    the very best milk for my baby.
Please watch over my son as he grows, Lord.
Help him to be strong and healthy.
Surround us with Your peace, that we might grow
    strong in Your love.
Thank You.
Amen.

### Being Grace

*As I nurse you, my son,*
*I know that I am no martyr,*
        *no savior,*
           *no saint.*
*I give no more than I am able.*
*Yet, miraculously, all that you are*
*has been made from what I have given.*

*I am a land of milk, if not honey.*

*Still, there was no sacrifice.*
*There is no debt.*

*These months have been our Holy Communion.*
*Take.*
*Eat.*
*This is my body.*

*I am poured out*
*for your small, hungry mouth*
*and perfect hands.*

*We are the two who gathered.*

*This is my body.*
*This is grace.*
*Take.*
*Eat this.*

---

*Don't give up. Raise it up in prayer.*

## A Prayer for Help in Breastfeeding

Dear God,

Help me to breastfeed my baby.

Give me the patience and health I need to persevere
    while I learn this new skill.

May my milk flow freely and easily in response
    to the needs of my baby.

Surround me with wise women who can
    teach and advise me.

Surround me with the support
    of encouraging words and smiles.

Give me faith and give me confidence.

I know that things will get easier as my baby and I
    learn this dance together.

Thank You, Lord.

Amen.

A Prayer for When Breastfeeding Is Not Working

Dear God,

I have done all that I can to breastfeed my baby.

I have talked with experts, I have worked with
    nurses and my doctor, I have read books, I have
    drunk water, I have tried medications, and I
    have pumped.

Breastfeeding is just not working
    for my baby and me.

I am so disappointed, Lord.

I feel that I have failed.

I feel the judgment of others and the harsh criticism
    of my own mind.

Comfort me, Lord, as I comfort my baby.

Take my judgment and bring me peace.

Take my feelings of failure and
    show me my successes.

Wrap Your light around my baby and me
    and guide us forward.

Thank You.

Amen.

---

*I am the best authority on my baby.*
*I trust my instincts, and I trust my baby.*

## A Prayer for Pumping

Dear God,
Please be with me as I express this milk to
    feed my baby.
Thank You, Lord.
Amen.

I love the term "expressed milk." It seems an appropriate way to recognize that we express our love and devotion to our children through this process.

I pumped every three hours until Clayton was strong enough to nurse. On the one hand, I was grateful for the machines that helped me to feed my baby. On the other, I felt like I was being "milked."

At first, I found it hard to relax. The process was painful, and the incessant wheeze of the machine seemed eternal. Then one morning I matched the repetitive in and out wheeze of the pump with the words, "Thank You, Thank You, Thank You" and "God bless, God bless, God bless."

Soon I found that these mantras could take me to a place of peace. Despite the pain of pumping, I relaxed, which helped my milk production and helped the time to pass.

## A Prayer for Formula Feeding

Dear God,
Grant me wisdom in choosing
    the right formula for my baby.
Bless those who created it,
    and bless me as I prepare it.
May the light of Your love fill every bottle and help
    my baby to grow strong and healthy.
Thank You, Lord.
Amen.

❧

When to wean is a highly controversial topic. As a new mother, I was curious as to how other mothers handled the situation. I craved their stories and guidance. I offer my process here not because my way is the only way or the right way, but because it is one story in the millions of stories that we all need to hear and to tell.

I knew that I wanted to nurse for at least a year. This seemed a lofty goal when I was transferring Clayton from the bottle-feeding of the NICU to my breast. He would go rigid and scream every time I offered to nurse. Forcing a screaming baby onto my breast was not the idyllic picture of nursing I had held in my imagination, but it was how we began. I learned to spray some formula into his mouth and then onto my breast and then quickly latch him on. This trick eventually worked, and we were on our way.

I loved breastfeeding. Once established, it was much easier than trying to get up at night to prepare formula. However, I was never able to produce enough milk to pump ahead, which meant that no one could feed him but me. After a year of breastfeeding, I was ready to begin the weaning process.

I had always nursed on demand. After a year, I began to not offer, but not deny Clayton if he wanted to nurse. My husband began getting up with Clayton at the break of day and giving him some milk to replace the first morning nursing. A few weeks later, I was nursing only once or twice a day and once at night.

When Clayton was hospitalized at fourteen months with hemolytic uremic syndrome (HUS, which I will talk more about later), we went back to full nursing on demand to get him through. Once he was well again, I repeated the above process; within a month or so, we were down to only night nursing. When it got to ten minutes a night as our only nursing, I began to cut our night session back by one minute each week and I sang to him more. The week that we got down to two minutes of nursing a night and two songs, Clayton refused the breast and we were done. It was a bittersweet end, but I was ready and he never looked back. I found that I had a bit of the "baby blues" for a couple of weeks after Clayton was weaned, and it took about a month for my hormones to fully regulate themselves so that I felt like I was back to normal.

I remember a mother asking me if Clayton had initiated weaning. I didn't know what to say. I have always considered my relationship with my son to be a dynamic conversation. If I was ready to be done with nursing and had already nursed for eighteen months, I did not think it was necessary to wait for him to be the full decision maker in our relationship. I was ready to be done at a year and he probably would have nursed longer if I had encouraged it. I felt that we had found a suitable compromise where we were both satisfied.

Whether you choose to wean in the first year or much later on, prayer is a helpful accompaniment.

## A Prayer for Weaning

Dear God,

The time has come for my child to wean.

Please guide us in this process.

Surround me with helpful information
    and wise guides.

Make me so fluent in the language of loving care
    that my baby transitions easily.

I ask that You watch over my body
    as it regulates itself.

Help me through the hormonal changes that
    accompany this shift and keep me healthy,
    balanced, and mentally clear.

Grant me patience with this process, Lord.

Thank You.

Amen.

## A Prayer for Starting Solid Foods

Dear God,

My baby is growing so quickly.

I ask Your guidance in making healthy food choices
for my family.

Lord, it seems that so many of the foods offered to
us are created without regard for health.

Please help me to find those
that are truly nourishing.

Help me to be a good example, Lord.

Guide me to food that feeds and sustains us well.

Please watch over us.

Thank You, Lord.

Amen.

> *When people ask me what I do, I now answer*
> *"I mother, and I pray."*

## A Prayer for Vaccinations

Dear God,

Please wrap Your arms around my child and
    bless the vaccine he is about to receive.

Bless the nurse who gives it
    and those who created it.

Please make this process as painless as possible
    and grant me peace as I hold my baby.

Thank You for gently bringing the power of this
    medicine to his body.

May it make him strong and keep him well.

May the golden light of Your divine love
    surround us, keep us healthy,
    and grant us peace.

Thank You.

Amen.

Oliver Wendell Holmes said that a mind, once
stretched, never regained its original dimensions. After
pregnancy, I wondered if the same were true of my
belly and breasts.

## A Prayer for the Transitioning Body

Dear God,

The body that I now inhabit seems strange to me.

I ache where I once was strong.

Help me, Lord, to embrace and love the

    incredible flexibility of this body.

What a miracle that life was created within me.

Inspire me to take care of myself

    during this time of transition.

Help me heal. Help me grow.

Grant me patience.

Thank You.

Amen.

## A Prayer to Mend One's Self-image

Dear God,

Please help me to mend my image of myself.

In this moment my body seems strange

and unfamiliar to me.

Where I see destruction, show me a temple.

Where I see weakness, show me my strength.

Where I see scars, show me

the relics of my initiation.

Grant me Your eyes, Lord, that I may see

the beautiful and transformed woman I am

and that I am becoming.

Thank You.

Amen.

CHAPTER 6:

*I Remember Sleeping*

There was a time when I once believed wholeheartedly that I needed ten hours of sleep a night in order to function. After I became a mother, I learned that I really only needed four.

I was shocked when Clayton was only a few weeks old and people would ask me, "Is he sleeping through the night?" I always answered, "Are you kidding? He is up every two hours!" I didn't realize that some people thought a baby sleeping through the night was a sign of "good mothering." Other mothers, who were taken aback by my honesty, would lean in conspiratorially and whisper, "Mine never did either."

Why would we consider the well-rested mother with a baby who sleeps through the night to be a better mother than the one who spends the night caring for her baby? All babies have different needs. Mine needed me every two hours, and I complied not because my little baby "got me up," but because that was the way I chose to mother him.

If you have a good sleeper, you are blessed. If you have a colicky baby, you are blessed. If you have a frequent nurser or a "high needs" baby, you are blessed.

If you are getting the sleep you need, say a prayer of gratitude, and if you are not, be comforted in knowing that you are doing all that you need to do to take good care of your child.


A Nighttime Blessing 🎼

Angels full of love and light,
Come down around this house tonight.
As we sleep and as we dream,
Please hold us in your golden gleam.

Angels full of golden light,
Come down into our hearts tonight.
As we dream and as we sleep,
Please hold us in your love complete.
Amen.

Sleep deprivation took a real toll on me. I felt incapable of communicating with the rest of the world in a way that was effective and coherent. It was frightening to have to search for words that seemed to evaporate as I spoke.

My husband got very good at calming my fears and interpreting my random (and vehement) new combinations of sign language and gibberish: "It is next to the thing on the round red over there!"

Who am I? What have I become? I was terrified I would never recover.

## A Prayer for Patience with Sleep Deprivation

Dear God,
It seems that I have lost control over the words
    that I used to master.
Sentences and thoughts refuse to form,
    and I feel so lost and alone.
Conversations that used to be so easy are now trials
    as I struggle to find the words that escape
    my grasp.
I know that this is not forever, Lord.
Please grant me patience.
Transformation is happening before my eyes
    and within my soul.
There are no words,
    and my emotions overwhelm me.
Cradle me, Lord.
Rock me in Your loving arms as my baby and I
    grow into the loving and light-filled beings
    You would have us be.
Thank You.
Amen.

To this day, as I leave my son to sleep, I silently ask,
*Angels, please come down around Clayton and help him to sleep. Thank You. Amen.* It comforts me to know that I am not doing this alone.

## A Prayer to Help My Baby Sleep

Dear God,
Please send Your angels to wrap their wings
    around my baby and help him to sleep in
    the warmth of Your light.
May they sing to him their sweetest songs
    and guide him with peaceful dreams.
Thank You.
Amen.

The cruelest joke of all was that once Clayton began sleeping through the night (at ten months), I was so used to getting up that I could not sleep!

## A Prayer to Help Me Sleep

Dear God,

My baby is sleeping.

I am not.

Surround me with the warmth of Your peace.

Release me from my worries.

Cradle me in the light of Your love.

Thank You.

Amen.

# CHAPTER 7:

## Transition and Transformation

When I was pregnant, everyone told me that *my life* would change forever. No one ever told me that *I* would be forever changed. No one even hinted at how challenging this transformation might be.

I found early motherhood to be both a profound honor and a social demotion. As an older mother—I was thirty-five when my son was born—I had been independent for quite some time. I had worked for many years, gone to graduate school twice, and traveled the world. I was used to being an active person and a real "go getter." I relished moving fast and getting things done, and I took great pleasure in stimulating conversations and discussions with other adults.

My first few months as a mother, I was forgetful. It seemed I could never complete anything; I could not put two coherent sentences together, let alone have an intelligent discussion; and I was the most dependent I had been since I was young myself. On marathon nursing days, I would sit on the couch and make a list of all the things I was going to do as soon as I was able to move again. Getting to and through the grocery store seemed a monumental task. Dinner on the table was a minor miracle.

Eventually, I slowed down and realized all that I was getting done. I knew my baby. I knew him well. I served him well. The world was a more wondrous place because I had him to show it to. I relaxed more, I laughed more, and I accepted that I was transforming. I posted a sign in my kitchen: "Good mothers do not have clean houses!" My old self would never have said that. Now it is my motto, and I am sticking to it.

## A New Mother's Prayer

Dear God,

I feel overwhelmed with the responsibility
    of all the decisions I am to make.

Speak to me, Lord; be my guide.

Where I have doubts, send me confidence.

Where I hold worry, grant me peace.

I am just getting to know this little soul.

There are times I feel so frightened.

Wrap Your arms around me, Lord.

Send Your angels to our side.

Whisper in my ear and grant me Your wisdom.

Thank You.

Amen.

I think at some point every new mother must look around and say, "Oh my! This is my life?!" Dreaming about having a baby, taking care of others' children, and watching others raise their children is almost no preparation for the moment your own child is placed into your arms. Before you are a mother, it is easy to underestimate how difficult, time-consuming, and even life-consuming it can be to be a good mother.

I think most of us believe that even though others might have a hard time, we would somehow magically do it differently. I know I did. *For us, it will be easier,* I thought. There was even a time after Clayton got out of the hospital and we were home when I remember saying to my husband Tim, "This is easier than I thought it would be."

At that point Clayton slept most of the time, and I was beginning to see a rhythm developing. I could stare at him all day. He was absolutely the most beautiful, most precious blessing in my life.

A few months later, he was still my most precious blessing. He was still my beautiful boy. But he was no longer sleeping, and I struggled to find his new rhythm. I felt incapable even though I knew I was doing my best.

I began to crave just a few minutes in the shower alone. I yearned to do something that could be completed and put away so that I felt some sense of achievement. Even though I did not want to leave my baby, it was tempting to believe that I should be doing something else.

I had no idea what that something else would be, but surely there was something at which I was capable of succeeding, something that had immediate rewards.

It is easy to discount your impact as a mother. The fruits of mothering may not be seen for many years. During moments of uncertainty, I was not sure I was accomplishing anything.

The paradox of new motherhood is that you expect to be "busy," and you are, but it is not the busyness of pre-motherhood. It is not the busyness of rushing around and getting things done. It is instead a busyness of observation and attention, of focus and intention.

It is not that you "have no time," but that your time is full. Each moment is utterly and completely consumed with witnessing, honoring, and serving this new little being.

It took time for me to see that I was working miracles. It took time for me to see that I was setting the foundation for my son's life. It took time for me to be able to slow down and see that mothering is weaving the world. Mothering is forming the future. These times are precious gifts. These are sacred moments.

> *Although there are many things I am capable of doing right now, I will not be tempted to believe that any of them are more important than what I am doing in this moment—taking care of my child.*

## A Prayer for Help in Slowing Down

Dear God,
Help me to find comfort in a slower pace of life
    that is more in sync with my baby.
Show me the reverence born of each
    and every moment.
I am surrounded, Lord, by a "hurry up" world
    where I used to move with speed to succeed.
My very body rebels at this new rhythm.
Yet it is the rhythm of the trees.
It is the rhythm of the waves.
It is the rhythm of my blood
    as it moves surely forward.
There is time.
I breathe it in.
I hold it gently in my own small hands.
Thank You.
Amen.

---

*I am divinely loved.*

---

## A Prayer for Patience

Dear God,
I feel like the time I used to call my own
    will never be mine again.
Yet I know that all things change.
My baby will grow, and so will I.
Help me to embrace this time in my life with joy
    and an open heart.
Thank You, Lord.
Amen.

---

*This too shall pass.*

---

My New Year's resolution as a new mother was that I would not say anything to or about myself that I would not say to or about my son. As a new mother, I was my greatest critic.

When I was tired, I called myself "foolish" and sighed with exasperation whenever I forgot something. I was impatient with my body and critical of my appearance. My resolution helped me to change those behaviors and be more forgiving and accepting of who I was.

If we wish our children to respect and love themselves, we must be their example.

## A Daily Blessing

Dear God,

Please bless my hands with gentle kindness.

Bless my mouth with words of encouragement
for myself and for my baby.

Bless my body with vitality and the energy
to do with joy what is required of me.

Bless my mind with positive thoughts
and enthusiasm.

Help me to choose love in every interaction.

Bless me with forgiveness and perseverance
when I fall short of my own expectations.

My hands are Your hands, Lord.

Bless them that all around me might be blessed.

Thank You.

Amen.

## A Daily Prayer

Dear God,
Please wrap Your arms around me and help me
    to be the mother You would have me be.
When things are chaotic, make me a center of calm.
When I am bored, show me the wonder in my child
    and in the world.
When I am tried and tired,
    bless me with kindness and patience.
Lord, grant me Your eyes, Your enthusiasm,
    Your love.
My eyes are Your eyes.
My hands are Your hands.
My heart is Yours.
May it bless my family and the world.
Thank You.
Amen.

There are so many times when mothering is truly blissful: first smiles, baby giggles, a caress that is just for you.

During those wondrous moments with your child, take a deep breath and say out loud, "This is a beautiful moment." By "calling out" these moments, you are more likely to recall them later.

A Prayer of Gratitude for the Magic of Mothering

Dear God,
Thank You for this wonderful,
    magical moment with my child.
Please plant this experience deep in my heart as a
    touchstone that I can call on when I forget
    the grace that surrounds my life.
I am blessed to be here.
Thank You, Lord.
Amen.

Recalling these moments is important when times are not as easy. Looking into the eyes of your child and finding the face of God is easier to do when he is smiling than when he just threw up all over you as you were on your way out the door.

I find it helpful, when things are trying, to envision Clayton grown up and watching from a far corner of the room. I imagine him saying: "Wow! You were so patient with me!" "Wow! You were so much fun!" "Wow! You are such a great mother!" In that moment I know that I am all of those things, and I believe that Clayton knows I am, too.

*Even in the midst of chaos,*
*there is a center of reverence.*
*Breathe deeply into that space.*
*Here you are held.*
*Here you are whole.*
*Here you are renewed.*
*Here you are transformed.*

In trying times, the most profound prayer is often the simplest.

Help me, Lord.
Thank You.
Amen.

When times are hard, nothing helps more than a sense of humor. I try to imagine myself telling one of my friends about a particular incident and laughing about it. If you will look back on something in five years and laugh about it, why not laugh about it now?

## A Prayer to Appreciate the Humor in Life

Dear God,
I am willing to see the blessing in this moment
    (or at least the humor).
Please, Lord, open my eyes.
Thank You.
Amen.

For those times when we do not quite meet the
standards that we set for ourselves, there is always the
comfort of prayer.

## A Prayer for When We Fall Short

Dear God,

I have fallen short of my own expectations,
   and I cannot rest.

Help me, Lord.

Show me how to move past and learn from
   this experience.

I know that with Your guidance I can be the mother
   you mean for me to be.

Open my heart to Your love.

Open my mind to Your inspiration, to Your words.

Please, show me the way of forgiveness.

I give this burden to You, Lord.

Take it and transform it.

Thank You.

Amen.

The way that we perceive ourselves as mothers matters.
If we feel burdened, our children will feel like burdens.
If we feel blessed (though sometimes stressed), our
children will know that they are cherished.

## A Prayer for When Feeling Stressed

Dear God,

Help me to see with Your eyes.

When I feel stressed, show me that I am blessed.

When I feel overwhelmed, clear my way.

Help me to find a community of support so that
I know I am not alone.

Show me the path of joy so that I may choose it
today and every day.

Thank You, Lord.

Amen.

When Clayton was a baby, my husband's work often took him away from us for long days and long trips. I found prayer to be a great comfort when he was away.

## A Prayer to Watch over a Loved One

Dear God,

Please watch over my husband as he travels.

Please send Your mightiest angels to

    watch over him and keep him safe

    while he is away from us.

Sustain me, Lord, while he is gone.

Grant me patience, peace, clarity, and strength.

Wrap my family in the light of Your love

    until we are together again.

Thank You, Lord.

Amen.

When a child is sick, even with a routine illness, it can feel all-consuming to a new mother.

A Prayer for When a Baby Is Sick

Dear God,
Please come down around my baby and
    restore him to perfect health.
Show me how best to care for him
    during this time of illness.
Bless my hands with Your healing light
    and surround me with guiding angels
    as we recover.
Thank You.
Amen.


Motherhood does not simply change our lives. It is more profound than that: it changes who we are as people. It transforms our bodies, our minds, and our way of thinking; it changes how we act and how we relate to the world in which we live.

When we choose to approach motherhood as a sacred calling and spiritual practice, we elevate the effort it demands to the level of sacrament.

We are the vessel.
We are the hymn.
We are the prayer.
We are the blessing.
Amen.

CHAPTER 8:

*Unexpected Entrances — Prayers for the*
*Neonatal Intensive Care Unit*

Our son Clayton spent the first two weeks of his life in the neonatal intensive care unit (NICU). The day that we were cleared to leave, one of the doctors turned to us and said, "You have a healthy baby now." I burst into tears of gratitude. "I have a healthy baby now" became my mantra. *I have a healthy baby now… Clayton is a healthy baby… I have a healthy baby…*

I often include the parents of sick children in my prayers. Nothing brings you to your knees faster than a child who is seriously ill. It changes you. Each little cold brings me to battle with my fears. *Is it something more? Am I missing something?* Then I remember my mantra: *I have a healthy baby now.* I repeat it over and over. *I will not infect my son with my own fear. I have a healthy baby now. He is strong. He is healthy. Dear God, please watch over my son.*

*A Perfect Day*

*The day you were born was a perfect day.*
*For although there were fears and emergencies,*
*There were also angels and grace.*

*Your perfect blue eyes, looking back at me through the glass*
*and distance, assured me that you were really here.*

*And though your lungs needed encouragement, your spirit*
*was strong and calm and so trusting as we poked and*
*prodded you toward perfect health.*

*We held you gingerly and fiercely close to our hearts.*

*And now you are strong.*
*And now you are wise.*
*And now you laugh with open arms, embracing the world.*

*As you grow, I will carry this lesson with me:*
*Where there is fear, there is also grace.*
*Where there are emergencies, there are also angels.*

*Sometimes all a mother can do is breathe deeply and pray.*

A Prayer for a Family with a Premature Baby

Dear God,
Our baby was in a hurry to be at our side,
    eager to be here on Earth.
Please grant him the courage and strength he needs
    to get through this hospitalization.
Bless the hands of every person who touches him.
Bless the medicines and machines that are helping
    him stay here with us.
Bless those who research and develop those
    medicines, machines, and protocols.
We are so grateful, Lord.
Send us Your angels to guide us, and surround our
    baby with the light of love and healing.
Calm our hearts and minds and clarify our thoughts
    as we make decisions for our child.
Help us to see the wisdom of this path.
We would not have chosen it for ourselves.
We surrender and give this situation to You, Lord.
Take our fear and bring us calm.
Take our fear and bring us love.
We ask You for a miracle today, Lord.

Heal our baby.
Heal our family.
Grant us peace.
Thank You.
Amen.

Clayton's birth taught me that I cannot control
what happens. All I can control is how I choose to
understand the situation. I did not know how things
would turn out, but I did know that there were
big angels all around me as I was whisked into the
emergency room the day he was born.

I was blessed with a doctor who was at the top of his
field, and I was blessed with nurses who were gentle,
caring, and considerate. I was blessed to have my
mother by my side, and I was blessed by the small,
bleating sound my son made as he began his earthly
existence. I would not see him for hours and would
not hold him until the next day, but in that small
sound, I heard hope, I heard answered prayers, and
I heard the strong will of a little boy determined to
be here.

## A Prayer for Understanding

Dear God,

This is not the journey I had planned.

Help me to see the blessings of this path.

I give You my fear.

I ask for Your grace.

Sustain me, Lord.

Give me strength.

Surround my family and me with Your angels,

    and guide us through this time of difficulty.

Bless all those who are to help us

    along this new way forward.

Thank You.

Amen.

The day Clayton was born, my husband made a hasty return from a business trip, arriving in time to see our son being loaded into an ambulance bound for another hospital forty-five miles away. He checked on me and then followed our son to the other hospital. There he learned all about the monitors and machines Clayton was hooked up to, he learned all about protocols, and he held our little boy's hand all night long until Clayton was breathing in a more predictable way. He played a CD of my voice so that Clayton would know that we were all still together, and he prayed.

Throughout our NICU stay, I was grateful that I had a recording of my voice. It calmed Clayton when we were not able to be with him.

The following is a script that you could record to be played to your baby in the case of an early birth. Of course, anything that you say or sing will be a wonderful gift. Envision your baby well and in your arms. Still your fears and use your voice to inspire his confidence. Your child will love to hear the familiar cadence of your words and songs in the midst of the beeps and mechanics of any NICU.

> Hello Little One,
> We are so happy that you are here. We have only just met, and yet we love you so much. You are so brave. This is not an easy entrance into the world, but we are going to do all that we can to make it better for you. Rest easy, sweetheart. You need to rest and grow. You are in our hearts and our thoughts every minute of the day. You are surrounded by

miracle workers, and you are surrounded
by angels. Rest easy. We love you. Rest.

For days after Clayton was born, I had phantom
movements in my uterus. I would turn to Tim and say,
"He just kicked." And then I would realize, of course,
that was impossible. It took a few days for my body to
catch up to what had happened. I remember saying
sadly, "My baby is here [meaning he had been born],
but my baby is not *here* [in my arms]."

## A Prayer for When You and Your
## Baby Are Separated

Dear God,

I feel so lost and so sad.

I just want to hold my baby.

Please, God, wrap us in the light of Your love.

Hold me and hold my baby in Your arms until we are
together again.

Please bless my new family.

Thank You.

Amen.

Clayton's time in the hospital introduced me to a new kind of strength. It was excruciating to not be able to hold my baby whenever I wanted. There were so many tests and procedures and things to monitor that I had to surrender to protocols and trust the experts around us.

There were times when we did speak up, and we were right to do so. The doctors and nurses were wonderful, but they were responsible for a ward of newborns, and we had only one baby to watch over.

## A Prayer for Help with Protocols

Dear God,
Help me to know when to honor protocols
    and when to advocate for my child.
Help me with the decisions I am to make.
Clear my mind.
Make me strong.
Help me, Lord.
Thank You.
Amen.

While I was recovering in the NICU, a well-meaning social worker suggested that I would need "to mourn the birth that I did not have." I think this kind of focus on birth is dangerous. I did everything I could have done to have a natural birth, but in the end, birth is not about what a mother wants. Birth is not about the mother. Birth is about *becoming* a mother.

The notion put forth in many birthing books that birth is to women what war is to men warrants rethinking. I do not believe that either giving or taking life should serve as a proving ground for one's own self-worth. Birth should not be made into a competition.

When you become a mother, you do what is best for your child.

I will never forget the times I overheard Tim talking to others about our birth experience. "The nurse said she had never in all her years seen anything like it! The worse things got, the more Amy relaxed, which helped everyone involved. She did such a great job. My wife is an amazing woman."

The nurse's comments to my husband and my husband's obvious pride meant the world to me and provided me with a positive framework from which to understand my experience.

My actions and conduct saved both my life and that of my son. To mourn not having everything the way I originally wanted it would be to reject the lessons that our birth brought.

A Prayer for Acceptance

Dear God,

I ask that You open me to the blessings of situations
that are out of my hands.

Help me to learn the lessons that will enrich my life.

I give You any disappointment.

I ask for Your grace.

I give You my insecurities.

I ask for Your confidence.

Please make meaning of this experience for me.

Help me to grow as a mother from what
I have learned.

Please make of this experience a miracle.

Thank You.

Amen.

In the first few days that Clayton was in the NICU, he went through a battery of tests. The actual names and procedures that were done are now lost to me in the heavy haze of those first few days. However, there is one moment that I recall clearly.

The day that they were scheduled to test to determine brain function, I remember the following thoughts flowing through my head: *If my son is disabled, I hope that no one ever says, "I'm sorry," because he will always be perfect in my eyes. If others are unable to see his perfection, it will be because of their disability, not that of my son. If Clayton is unable to see his perfection, it will be my job to show him. His form will help to inform his life. All will be well with my son.*

## A Prayer for My Baby

Dear God,

As my baby grows, I ask You to find ways

to let him know that he is a well-loved

and important part of this world.

Lord, help him to find and embrace the divine spark

You place in each and every one of us.

We are all blessed with a divine purpose.

Lead my child, Lord.

Lead our family.

Take our hands.

Thank You.

Amen.

## A Prayer for the Parents of a Special-Needs Baby

Dear God,

Show me the beauty and perfection in my child.

Make his light shine so clearly, Lord,

    that he may find only his beauty

    reflected in my eyes.

Open my heart to the lessons that

    raising my son will bring.

Open my life to all those who will come to guide

    me and share in this journey.

Be with us as we face every challenge.

Be with us as we celebrate every milestone.

Be with us and fill our family with Your love.

May we be a shining example

    as we learn and grow together.

Thank You.

Amen.

## A Prayer for an Enlightened World

Dear God,
Help me to forgive those
    who judge my child unfairly.
Take my resentment.
Give me Your peace.
Remind me that the wounds of others
    are what keep them from seeing my child in
    the full light of his being.
Illuminate their hearts, Lord.
Light the world.
Thank You.
Amen.

Our time in the NICU introduced me to true heroism.
The doctors and nurses are miracle workers, but
the unsung heroes are the parents. There is no way
to prepare yourself to hear that your baby is sick,
that your baby needs an operation, that your baby is
disabled, or that your baby may not live. Each test or
surgery is met with courage. Each day is a test of faith.

Many parents were squeezed between their need to
work and their deep desire to be near their babies.
Some parents had already lost a child and were in the

NICU with another who was sick. Mothers pump and prepare formula around the clock, and fathers stand vigil by their child's bedside.

I was never more grateful for the gift of my husband than I was in the NICU. My family lives in a rural area, which means that our local county hospital performed the emergency work, but the facilities and critical care that Clayton needed were forty-five miles away at the major medical center. Clayton was rushed away as soon as he was stabilized while I had to wait for twenty-four hours to join him because of my blood loss and surgery.

The wait seemed like forever. Finally, the hour arrived, and I was transported by ambulance to join my family. Tim and I had talked earlier in the day, and I knew he'd been up all night and was exhausted. But when the attendants opened the back of the ambulance, there stood my husband with his dazzling smile and an armful of roses. He was wearing a newly purchased, brightly painted Hawaiian shirt and had taken care of all the arrangements for me as well as those for Clayton.

Having a positive and loving partner in this world is a gift beyond measure, a true blessing. Tim's Hawaiian shirts quickly became legend in the NICU, and we now celebrate Clayton's birthdays with "Birthday Luaus." Clayton has inherited his father's love of this exotic garb. The first shirt he ever chose for himself was a bright blue Hawaiian.

## A Prayer for Those Who Support Us

Dear God,

My (husband) is a gift beyond measure.

I am so grateful.

To have him by my side is to live
    in the palm of Your hand.

Grant us patience and understanding as we move
    through this trying time.

Keep our spirits light and our hearts open as we
    listen for Your guiding voice.

May these challenges bring us ever closer in love.

May we serve each other
    and keep each other strong.

May we find hope in each other's eyes
    and faith in each other's hands.

Hold us, Lord.

Thank You.

Amen.

## A Prayer for Mothers in Need of Support

Dear God,

Send me your angels of calm and comfort.

Open my eyes to those around me who are working
as Your hands, Lord.

Lift me up and hold me in the light of Your love.

Send me the help that I need in this trying time.

Keep me strong.

Stand with me.

Lead me on.

Thank You.

Amen.

After two weeks in the NICU, we were finally able
to spend the night together as a family. Tim and I
cuddled up in the single hospital bed and listened
to our son breathe in and out on his own. What a
precious and beautiful sound. The next day we were
going home! After weeks of being surrounded by
doctors and nurses, we were both excited and nervous
to be leaving the hospital.

## A Prayer for Leaving the NICU

Dear God,
We are so grateful to be taking our baby home.
Thank You for this incredible mircle
    and blessing in our lives.
Our minds know that we have a healthy baby, Lord.
But our hearts are afraid.
Please erase all thoughts of illness or fear from our
    consciousness and fill us with Your light.
Grant us courage and confidence as we grow into
    the parents we are called to be.
Thank You, Lord.
Amen.

When a family leaves the NICU, they pray that they
will never have to go back. There are, however, no
guarantees. Whether a return to the NICU is needed
as a follow-up to care or for a completely new malady,
prayer can help you get through the door.

*Be with us, Lord. Lead us on.*

When Clayton was fourteen months old, he became
sick again. I tried not to be the much-maligned

"paranoid, overprotective mother." Clayton had bad diarrhea for a week and a fever. I kept taking him to doctors, but they could find nothing wrong. I convinced myself he was just teething. Then one morning he looked extremely pale. I told the doctor, "I am terrified that you are going to tell me he has leukemia." We had his blood drawn.

I took my baby home and walked through the door to the sound of the telephone ringing. It was our doctor. I heard the call in sound bites: We had been admitted to the children's hospital two hours away. We were to get there as soon as we could. Clayton's platelet numbers had plunged. There was a 90 percent chance it was leukemia and a 10 percent chance it was something else. If he had a seizure on the way to the hospital, we were to take him to the closest emergency room. I called my husband, I hit my knees, and I prayed.

I do not know what it is like to have a child with leukemia. I do, however, know what it is like to sit with doctors and begin discussing protocols for leukemia treatment.

About a day after we were admitted, one of the doctors came in and said that it seemed that Clayton's red blood cells were being replenished, something that does not happen with leukemia. Clayton was diagnosed with a very rare disorder called hemolytic uremic syndrome (HUS). A toxin had caused the destruction of his red blood cells. Though HUS is a life-threatening event, each day we watched his bone marrow work hard to replenish his platelet levels. One of the doctors said he had the strongest bone marrow they had ever seen. We were so proud!

Through it all, Clayton smiled at the doctors who came to take his blood and laughed at the balloons that filled his room. There is a classic picture from this time in which I am holding him as I talk with one of the nurses. I have a look of great concern on my face. Clayton is sticking his tongue out at the camera. A week later, he was released, and though he still had some recovery time ahead of him, he was strong and soon became well.

One year later, we marked our first full year without a "hospital vacation," and I was so grateful. I work hard to keep my worry at bay. I remind myself that routine colds and croup are all a part of growing up. I use the following prayer whenever Clayton is sick to remind me that he is a strong boy and that he will make it through the routine trials of childhood.

## A Prayer for Keeping Fears Away

Dear God,

Please be with me as I battle fears from my past.

My child is not feeling well.

This is a minor illness compared to what he has
already been through.

My mind knows that he will soon recover,
but my heart is afraid.

Keep me vigilant while stilling my fears.

Help me to be here now.

Surround us with the warm light of Your love.

Open us to the miracle of health and fill us with
Your strength.

Bless my hands that I may do Your work.

Bless my hands that they may bless my child.

Restore us all to perfect health.

Please Lord, hear my prayer.

Thank You.

Amen.

CHAPTER 9:

*Caretakers and Employment*

Having children has never been a money-making proposition. If it was, who would ever be crazy enough to apply for the job? Imagine a classified ad in the *Universal Times Herald.* It reads:

> ***A Good Mother****: Completely (or at least moderately) selfless, dedicated woman to commit body and soul for the teaching and development of co-soul in human infant form. Must be able to breathe deeply during times of crisis, change diapers (cloth preferred), engage in endless discussions about poop, and organize and administer feedings (breastfeeding preferred, all other sources to be organic and home-cooked if possible). Must be up-to-date with all child safety precautions and procedures and CPR certified.*
>
> *Must be able to anticipate even the craziest of actions by child(ren) in order to save them from themselves. Experience in singing a range of music from lullabies to improvisational melodies necessary to prevent meltdowns. Funny kitchen dances mandatory.*
>
> *Must be able to cheerfully get up at all hours on demand for nursing and/or other soothing. Must be able to cook, clean, make telephone calls, and order infant environment silently while child sleeps.*

*Will be held at least partially responsible for the development of said child until adulthood. Must not be anxious about this lest the child be unduly influenced. Must be able to maintain healthy relationships with other adults in order to set a good example for the child as he/she grows. Must also cultivate other personal interests so that her own Earth contract is fulfilled in full and take on work outside the home at times so that all ends meet.*

*Title: Mother. (Or whatever the child eventually decides to call you. Keep in mind that this title will change as he/she grows.)*

*Salary and Health Insurance: none.*

*Benefits: to be determined and commensurate with experience and maturation of souls involved.*
*Possible benefits include: unimaginable joy, sloppy kisses, and unexpected smiles and laughter.*

*Duration of contract: the rest of your life.*

*No experience necessary.*

"What do you do?" As a new mother who was staying at home, I grew to dread this question. Should I talk about the jobs I had held before I became a mother? They did not feel like an accurate representation of what I was doing. Should I anticipate what I would be doing for work in the future? I was not sure what that would be. I knew that becoming a mother had transformed me in a profound way and that it would also transform my work. My most honest answer would have been, "Laundry, mostly." But that felt flippant and disrespectful of all the love and effort I was putting into raising my son.

The first few times I was asked, I mumbled something incoherent about my old life and the degrees I had and realized how invested I was in being seen as an intelligent and capable person (which I certainly did not resemble at the time). Months later I simply told people, "I am a mom," and practiced observing their reactions.

Some were dismissive, some were interested, some were accepting, and some were judgmental. But I was finally comfortable. I didn't care so much about what others thought of me or how I was mothering or if I should or should not be working outside the home.

I knew that I would need to get back to work and that my time as a stay-at-home mother would change. I struggled with my path forward, but I was proud that I had one thing that would not change. I was a mom.

As mothers today, we are faced with many options and the judgment of those who choose differently. One mother with whom I arranged a playdate confessed that she was worried that I would cancel our meeting if I found out that she had already returned to work.

Our judgments of each other will not illumine the world.

We are all doing the best that we can, and none of us can do it alone. It was my struggle with my identity as a mother that brought me to motherhood as my spiritual practice. I knew that what I was doing was important and transformational, and it had me, heart and soul. Making the shift in my mind from motherhood as repetitive drudgery that was underappreciated to seeing my efforts as rituals of transcendence and transformation changed my life.

Mothering is not my job; it is my sacred creation and calling. It is my invitation to transformation and the foundation of my new life.

I was panicked the first time I left my son alone with my mother, but he did beautifully. I felt that I had had a glimpse of "empty-nest syndrome." It was as if I had left a part of my own body behind. But I needed to go. We all need breaks. God bless all those who help us to care for our children. God bless all those who help to care for us.

May God bless and surround you with meaningful work that feeds more than just a bank account. May you find a community of loyal and loving care.

## A Prayer for Protection

Dear God,
Please bless our family as we go about our day.
Surround us with wise and guiding angels.
May those of us who travel to do our work
    do so safely and return home safely.
May we all find inspiration and joy in our day
    and in each other.
Thank You.
Amen.

## A Prayer for When Working Is Hard

Dear God,

I must leave my child to go to work.

Please help me, Lord.

This is one of the hardest things I have ever
had to do.

Wrap Your arms around me, Lord.

Surround me with Your light.

Help me to do my work efficiently and wisely,
and speed me safely home.

Please, Lord, send me the best possible caregivers,
and bless them with Your love and wisdom as
they watch over my child.

My heart is breaking, Lord.

Please make the answers to all my new decisions
clear for me.

Send Your wisest angels to whisper in my ear and
counsel me on this journey.

I am blessed.

I am transforming.

Guide me to be the best mother I can be.

Thank You.

Amen.

## A Prayer for Combining Working and Mothering

Dear God,

Please be with me as I work.

Grant me the wisdom to do my work well.

Grant me a clear mind to do my work efficiently.

Grant me patience toward my coworkers and
　　with myself.

I am responsible for so much, Lord.

Help my baby to understand that my heart
　　is always with him and that he is deeply loved.

Wrap us all in Your loving embrace.

Thank You.

Amen.

## A Prayer of Gratitude for Work and Mothering

Dear God,

Thank You for the blessing of meaningful work.

I am so fortunate to have work that fulfills me and
lifts me up to be the person You would have
me be.

I ask Your continued guidance as I incorporate my
roles as mother and career person.

Show me the way, Lord.

All things are in perfect process, and I know that
my life is being transformed.

May every aspect of my life be richer for my
involvement in the others.

May my work and my mothering inform each other,
and may both be a blessing to the world.

Thank You.

Amen.

> *Joy is at the heart of every awakening.*

## A Prayer for Daycare

Dear God,
Please send Your angels down around
    my baby and this place.
Bless all the caregivers here with
    wisdom and patience.
Bless all the children who will come into contact
    with my baby and grant them joy.
Thank You.
Amen

It is heart-wrenching to drop a wailing child off at the home of a caregiver. I knew Clayton stopped crying the minute I was out of earshot, but the following prayer became a helpful transition ritual for us. I would kneel down, look him in the eyes, and sing this blessing to him as I called the angels down around him.

 As I Go

Angels before you,
Angels behind you,
Angels surround you
as you grow.

Angels before me,
Angels behind me,
Angels surround me
as I go.
Amen.

At the end, I would wave and leave. I was often surprised at the power of this little song to comfort and transition him to his new space.

It may seem impossible to believe right now, but someday your child will be happy to see you go! I can imagine that when Clayton goes off to college, I will be the one reciting the first stanza, and he will be reciting the second.

.

CHAPTER 10:

*Competition and Criticism*

You will run into mothers whose children were potty trained in the womb, whose children spoke in complete sentences before they could raise their own heads and who walked out of the uterus of their own accord. Congratulate and bless every one of them.

Dear God,
Please come down around us.
Grant me patience, love, enthusiasm, and support.
Bless us all as we do our very best to raise
    these wondrous beings who are our children.
Thank You.
Amen.

As a new mother it is hard to know if you are doing things "right." We all want gold stars, and there are just not that many being handed out. All children are different and develop at different rates. If we constantly seek approval for our mothering through the performance of our children, we risk making them like us rather than helping them become who they are meant to be.

Competition between mothers only encourages dishonesty and fear. Our children cannot tell us who we are; neither can we tell our children who they are. We are all learning and growing as individuals in relationship. This is the spiritual practice of parenting.

Dear God,
When I am tempted to compete with other mothers,
     remind me that I am the perfect mother
     for my child.
Show me the matchless glory of my child,
     that I may celebrate him and
     the unique beauty in every child.
Thank You.
Amen.

For some, there will always be a better way, and they are more than happy to share. Bless them and move on.

Dear God,
Please save me from the judgments of others.
Help me to find wisdom in their words
     if there is wisdom to be found.
If there is none, help me to move on quickly.
Light my way, Lord.
Thank You.
Amen.

CHAPTER 11:

*Looking Back and Moving Forward*

As I prepare this book to go to press, my son is a bit over three, he is potty trained, he just started preschool, and I am well rested. He is my joy.

While I used to think I would never have any creative time again, I now know that space opens up once more. I am writing and quilting and painting and performing, and that is also my joy.

I would not change one moment of Clayton's first years. I have learned things I never could have learned any other way, and I have emerged from his earliest childhood a calmer, more patient, joyful person.

Reading back over what I have written, I am tempted to wonder, *Was it really so hard? Why did I worry so much?* As a first-time mother, it was hard to see the rhythm of which I was a part. Difficult phases felt not like phases, but like the way motherhood would always be. Having passed through these first years, the choices that I made and the ramifications of those choices are much clearer. I know now what I could only take on faith as a new mother, and I have passed into that understanding a new person. I am transformed.

Motherhood is a slippery thing to talk about. Our memories reshape the past, the edges softened by the intense love we have for our children. When told, "Someday you will look back on these days and miss them," I knew that would be true for me. However, as a new mother, that knowledge was not helpful. We cannot live in a foreseen future. We live and are transformed by the now.

With that knowledge, I leave you with one final prayer and blessing.

May we learn to embrace the mundane as sacred.
May we find joy in the simplest of things.
May these words bring you peace.
May these words bring us understanding.
May our understanding birth a community.
May our community illumine the world.
Amen.

A Reader's Guide and Topics for Discussion

## Conception through Pregnancy

1) The author talks about how her desire for children changed over time. Was that true for you?

2) When did you decide that you wanted to be a mother?

3) How did you feel when you found out you would be a mother soon?

4) What was your biggest challenge in adopting or becoming pregnant? What did you learn from that experience? How will that new learning make you a better mother?

5) The author talks about her pregnancy taking on a new dimension once she could feel her baby move. When did your pregnancy or impending adoption feel "real" to you?

6) How did this period in your life affect you? Did you change any habits? Think differently? Wish or dream about new things? Did any new fears arise? How did you deal with these things?

7) What was your biggest challenge during this time? How did you deal with it? What did you learn?

## Labor and Birth

1) The author talks about planning for a natural birth. What did you assume about labor and birth or meeting your baby for the first time before it all happened?

2) How do you feel about the events surrounding the birth of your baby?

3) How do you feel about the social worker's suggestion that the author would need to "mourn the birth [she] did not have"?

4) The author talks about angels whispering in her ear concerning rushing to the hospital if she ever saw blood, and about the art project where she drew the face of a surgeon. Did you have any intuitions about your baby or the birth of your baby?

## Feeding and the Body

1) The author talks about her challenges in feeding her baby. What were your expectations about feeding your baby? How is the reality the same or different? What has surprised you about the choices around feeding your baby? What is your favorite moment?

2) The author talks about her feelings toward her body after the birth of her baby. If you became a mother through your own pregnancy did you feel differently about your body after giving birth?

3) How has becoming a mother affected how you think about your body? About women's bodies in general?

4) The author talks about how profoundly sleep deprivation affected her. Could you relate to that experience? What is/was your biggest sleep related challenge? Who is helping/helped you through this time?

## Becoming a Mother

1) What has been your proudest moment as a mother?

2) How has becoming a mother changed you? What do you think differently about?

3) Has being a mother changed your relationship with your own mother?

4) If your baby could talk, what wonderful things would he/she say about you? What gold star do you deserve? What do you do really well as a mother?

5) What is your biggest challenge right now? How has that changed over time? How do you see it changing in the future?

6) What are the beautiful moments that you "called out" today? This week? This month?

## Work, Home and Criticism

1) How do you feel about working outside the home or being a stay at home mother? Is this hard to discuss with other mothers who may or may not feel the same way you do? How might you overcome this challenge?

2) The author talks about feeling tempted to compete with other mothers. Have you felt that way? How did you deal with it?

3) The author talks about having the way she mothers criticized by others. Has this happened to you? Have you found some criticism hard to shake off? Why do you think it bothered you so much? Was any part of their criticism true?

4) The author states, "When talking to mothers about our lives we must find a balance between discouraging martyrdom and honoring the service of motherhood." How can we do that as mothers? How do you feel about the way the media deals with this topic?

## Spirituality and Mothering

1) The author calls mothering her spiritual practice. How do you feel about that perspective?
2) Do you agree with the author that becoming a mother is a rite of passage?
3) Do you pray?

## Perspective

1) The author talks about being able to see the repercussions of her choices only after coming out on the other side of the first transformative years of mothering. Could you relate to that statement? Do you think you will be able to relate to that statement in the future?

2) The author states: "If we seek approval for our mothering through the performance of our children, we risk making them like us rather than helping them to become who they are meant to be." Do you agree?

For more questions and topics for discussion, or to suggest your own, please go to www.transformationalmothering.com

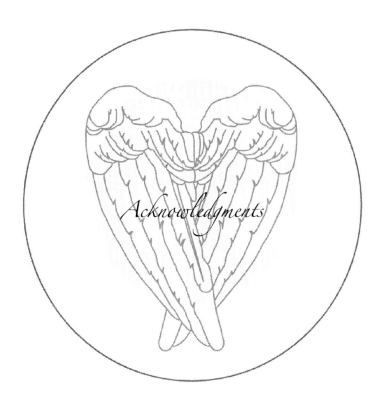

Acknowledgments

First thanks to God, who has blessed my life so abundantly. May this work be pleasing to You.

To the wondrous angels who watch over me, who guide my life, and who whisper in my ear—there are no words to express my gratitude. To be held in your wings is an ongoing miracle.

For all of the amazing people who read this book as it progressed and gave me clear, loving, and valuable feedback from first draft to final copy. My thanks to all of you!

To Michele Gray, who spent hours on the phone helping me sort through my thoughts and guiding me through the dark times—you are a light in my life.

To my first editor, Lane Fisher, who helped me through the tangled weeds of punctuation, and to the team at BookSurge who made this book polished and possible. Thank you for your precise and loving guidance.

To my husband Tim, who walks beside me, lifts me up, and clears my path. I am so grateful. I could not ask for a better partner.

And to my son Clayton. I thank you for being my wise teacher and my great joy. May you learn forgiveness from my mistakes. I love you—and I always will. You are a wonder.

About the Author

Amy Robbins-Wilson is an artist, writer, composer, and performer. A 1991 recipient of the Harry S. Truman Award for scholarship, leadership, and public service, she is committed to creating transformational spaces through the arts.

Ms. Robbins-Wilson holds a bachelor's degree in Empowerment Theater for Women from Bates College, a master's degree in Expressive Arts Therapies from Lesley University, and a second master's in Chant and Ritual Song Performance from The Irish World Academy of Music and Dance in Limerick, Ireland.

She makes her home in Maine with her husband, Tim, and their son, Clayton.

If you have questions or comments about this book Amy would love to hear from you!  Please contact her through her website at www.transformationalmothering.com.

While there you can read her blog, join our mailing list, get the musical downloads from the book and learn about Amy's new CD of prayers and lullabies, *The Divine Hours of Motherhood.*

*A portion of the proceeds generated by Amy's work is donated to the Children's Miracle Network and the Angelsong Endowment, which was established to benefit children and families in the Neonatal Intensive Care Unit. To learn more we invite you to visit www.angelsongendowment.org*

2273456

Made in the USA